Reptile Style

by Beth Gruber

Content Adviser: Professor Peter Bower, Barnard College, Columbia University, New York, New York
Reading Adviser: Frances J. Bonacci, Reading Specialist, Cambridge, Massachusetts

COMPASS POINT BOOKS

MINNEAPOLIS, MINNESOTA

Compass Point Books
3109 West 50th Street, #115
Minneapolis, MN 55410

Visit Compass Point Books on the Internet at *www.compasspointbooks.com*
or e-mail your request to *custserv@compasspointbooks.com*

Photographs ©: Ariel Skelley/Corbis, cover; Photos.com, 3; Corel, 4; Photos.com, 5 (top left); Clipart.com, 5 (top center left); Corel, 5 (bottom center left); James L. Amos/Corbis, 5 (bottom left); Photos.com, 7, 8; PhotoDisc, 9; Clipart.com, 10; Photos.com, 11; PhotoSpin, 12, 13; PhotoDisc, 14, 15; Clipart.com, 16; Corel, 17 (top left); PhotoDisc, 17 (bottom); Photos.com, 18; PhotoSpin, 19; Corel, 20; Annie Griffiths Belt/Corbis, 21; Morton Beebe/Corbis, 22; PhotoSpin, 23; Corel, 24 (bottom left); Clipart.com, 24 (top right); Photos.com, 25 (left center); Clipart.com, 25 (top center); Photos.com, 26 (top left); PhotoDisc, 26 (bottom left); Ingram Publishing, 27 (top left); Photos.com, 27 (left center); PhotoDisc, 27 (bottom left); Clipart.com, 28 (top left), 28 (bottom left); Corel, 28 (top right), 28 (bottom right); Clipart.com, 29, 31.

Creative Director: Terri Foley
Managing Editor: Catherine Neitge
Editors: Sandra E. Will/Bill SMITH STUDIO and Jennifer VanVoorst
Photo Researchers: Christie Silver and Tanya Guerrero/Bill SMITH STUDIO
Designers: Brock Waldron, Ron Leighton, and Brian Kobberger/Bill SMITH STUDIO and Les Tranby
Educational Consultant: Diane Smolinski

Library of Congress Cataloging-in-Publication Data
Reptile style / by Beth Gruber.
p. cm. — (Pet's point of view)
ISBN 0-7565-0699-9 (hardcover)
1. Reptiles as pets—Juvenile literature. I. Title. II. Series.
SF459.R4G78 2004
639.3'95—dc22   2004003395

Table of Contents

"From *my* point of view!"

NOTE: In this book, words that are defined in Words to Know are in **bold** the first time they appear in the text.

Who Is Your Reptile?

Pet Profiles

You and Your Reptile

Animal Almanac

Prehistoric Beginnings

When you look at small lizards and other **reptiles** like the turtle and garden snake, it is hard to believe that we are distant relatives of the dinosaur, but we are! In fact, the word dinosaur was created from two Greek words: *deinos* meaning "fearfully great" and *sauros* meaning "lizard."

The earliest reptiles first appeared on Earth about 340 million years ago. We evolved from **amphibians,** but our unique ability to reproduce without having to return to water made it possible for us to adapt to life on land. Over millions of years, we evolved into four distinct **orders.**

Order	Examples	Habitats	Unique Characteristics
Squamata 5,700 species	lizards, snakes	Species in this order live in trees, in burrows, on land, and in water. They can adapt to many climates, from the balmy tropics to the frigid Arctic Circle.	While lizards have feet, eyelids, and ears, snakes have none of these features.
Chelonia 200 species	turtles, tortoises, **terrapins**	Chelonia live in a variety of habitats in tropical and temperate zones.	Chelonians are the only reptiles whose bodies are protected by hard shells.
Crocodilia 23 species	crocodiles, alligators, **gharials**	Species in this order live in and near water in warm areas around the world.	A crocodile has a triangular shaped head with a pointed snout or nose. Alligators have a broad, rounded snout; gharial snouts are long and thin.
Rhynchocephalia 2 species	**tuataras**	Both species of rhynchocephalia are native to New Zealand. They can survive in much colder climates than most reptiles can.	These species—both endangered—spend most of their lives in burrows and come out only at night to feed on insects.

Outside In

Almost all reptiles have dry, scaly skin that contains extra-sensitive **receptors** that help us recognize touch, pain, heat, and cold. Our skin is made of **keratin,** a material also found in humans' fingernails!

Our skeletons vary depending on our shape. For example, some of us—particularly snakes—have no legs. Others, like turtles, have a hard shell that protects the backbone and ribs. Like humans, we are vertebrates, meaning that we have a backbone. Unlike humans, however, we have bones that will grow for as long as we live. This means we can grow to be giant-sized if we survive in the wild or are well-kept as pets.

Also unlike humans, we grow new teeth as we lose or shed old ones. Regardless of our size, our teeth are sized for holding and sometimes killing our prey.

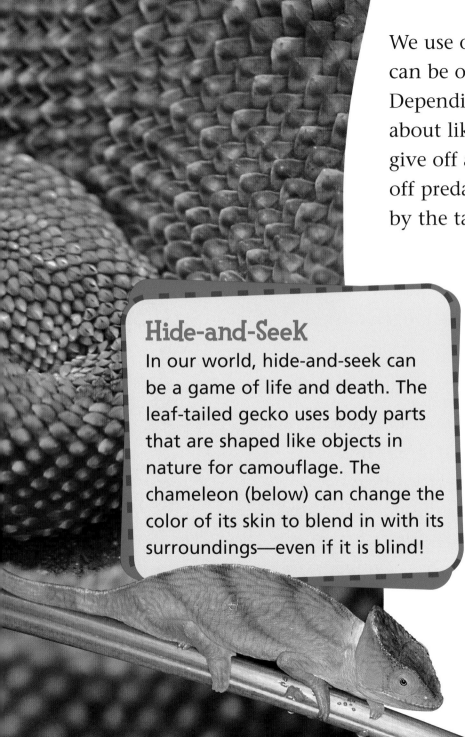

We use our tails to help us balance, and they can be our best defense when we are in trouble. Depending on the species, our tails can whip about like a powerful weapon, deliver poison, give off a smelly liquid substance that wards off predators, or even fall off if we are caught by the tail.

From the tiniest gecko to the mightiest crocodile, all reptiles are cold-blooded creatures. This means that our body temperature changes with our surroundings. We will bask in the sun to warm up and crawl under a rock to cool down. By moving back and forth between sun and shade, we keep our bodies at a surprisingly even temperature. As cold-blooded animals, we have very slow digestive systems and eat much less frequently than warm-blooded animals. If you were a reptile, you would only have to eat once a week!

Hide-and-Seek

In our world, hide-and-seek can be a game of life and death. The leaf-tailed gecko uses body parts that are shaped like objects in nature for camouflage. The chameleon (below) can change the color of its skin to blend in with its surroundings—even if it is blind!

The Detectors

Independent eye

Visible ear

Most reptiles rely on our senses of sight and smell, just like you do, and we have other ways of detecting things as well. Some of us depend on a single, well-developed sense to get around and avoid danger. Others use a combination of senses to navigate our worlds.

Except for those of us who live underground, most reptiles have good eyesight. However, because our eyes contain an extra color **cone,** we see the world very differently from humans. For example, while humans see a blue sky, we might see that same sky as green—or even some other color humans cannot even imagine!

Our range of vision depends on the position of our eyes. The tortoise, as well as many lizards, has eyes on either side of its head. A snapping turtle has eyes that face forward. A chameleon has eyes that swivel independently to see two views at once. Those of us who are **nocturnal** have smaller eyes than **diurnal** reptiles, and our pupils are large and slit-shaped to gather more light.

Many of us use our tongue, along with a sensory organ in the roof of our mouths called the **Jacobson's organ,** to smell, find food, and protect ourselves from predators. We use these organs in combination, much the way humans combine their senses of taste and smell.

Except for lizards, who have visible ears, most of us do not hear well. Lizards pick up airborne sounds better than snakes, who "hear" by feeling the ground shake. None of us can hear as well as a human, though.

Attacking the Music

For thousands of years, we snakes have been pictured dancing up and out of baskets to music being played on a pipe by snake charmers. If we can't hear well, how do we do it? We follow the movement of the pipe and rise up defensively in case we need to attack it.

The Inland Bearded Dragon

Real-Life Dragons

The world of reptiles is filled with many amazing species. When choosing a pet, though, you will want to narrow down your options to just a few kinds. Of the lizards, an inland bearded dragon—or "beardie"—like me is the easiest to care for. I make a great pet, especially for children and first-time pet owners. I am extremely docile and trusting. Even in the wild, people can walk right up to me to say hello. I rarely get upset, but when I do, you will see that I come by my name honestly. I can enlarge, or blow out, a flap of skin beneath my lower jaw until it looks like a beard!

I like to lie around all day in a nice warm cage with the temperature set to a toasty 85 degrees Fahrenheit (29 degrees Celsius). I am naturally curious and love to explore my environment.

Let me out of the cage, and I will run around the house until I find another warm spot in which to settle.

I eat insects, including mealworms, crickets, roaches, and waxworms. I also like chopped vegetables, such as collard greens, kale, turnip tops, and dandelion greens, as well as small pieces of squash, sweet potatoes, apples, and berries.

I am a native of Australia and can thrive in desert or woodland environments, but I like **savannas** best. When setting up my cage, choose things that resemble my natural habitat. Dried plants, a special reptile carpet made of smooth sand and gravel, and a water dish are a must. Add some large, smooth rocks for sunbathing and a limb for climbing, and I will feel right at home.

The Green Iguana

Jolly Green Giants

Are you patient and loving? Do you have time to train and play with me? If so, then a green iguana like me could be a great pet for you!

I come from the tropical rain forests of Central and South America. Unlike other lizards, I need plenty of love and human contact, just like a cat or dog. I like to be petted, talked to, and played with, and I need a regular routine to stay happy and healthy. I am not the kind of lizard that likes to lie around in a cage all day. In fact, I am a lot like a curious child—I want to explore everything, taste everything, and crawl into and up on every space imaginable. If you put me on a leash, you could even take me for a walk!

Green iguanas can grow to be 6 feet (2 meters) long, including the tail, and live to be 15 to 20 years old.

Since I am a wild animal, I need to be tamed, and taming me requires even more work than training a cat or a dog. I can sometimes be aggressive and might scratch you with my claws. However, if you learn how to handle me safely, interpret my signals, and give me room to roam inside and outside my cage, over time I will become a well-adjusted pet. I can even get along with the family cat or dog, if you introduce me slowly and carefully!

Third eye

Three-Eyed
In addition to my two obvious eyes, I also have a third eye on top of my head. It does not look like an eye, but it can detect movement and changes in light and dark.

The Leopard Gecko

Designer Lizards

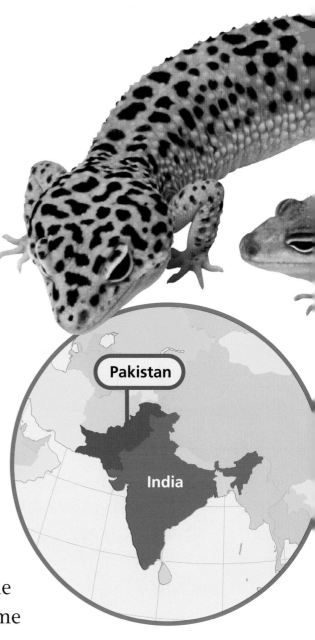

Few lizards, except perhaps the inland bearded dragon, are as easy to care for as me. I'm a leopard gecko. I never get larger than 7 to 10 inches (18 to 25 centimeters), so I am small enough for children to handle with supervision. I can have many different colors and patterns, and I am happy to be left alone most of the day.

I am originally from Pakistan and India, but I have been bred in **captivity** for generations. Captive breeding helps get rid of my natural wild instincts and makes it possible for humans to take me home, set up my habitat, and just plain love me.

When I am a baby, I am fidgety and excitable but totally harmless. As an adult, I am so tame that I will take food from a person's fingers.

Pakistan

India

If you keep a leopard gecko like me as a pet, you had better like bugs a lot—especially crickets and mealworms. I eat four live bugs daily, and before I eat them, you will have to fatten them up by letting them swim around overnight in a jar of water that has been fortified with vitamin powder and a carrot!

No Kissing!

It is a good thing I do not look very kissable, because you should never kiss a reptile. Reptiles like me carry salmonella, the same infection you can get from eating spoiled food, like potato salad at a picnic. You will also need to wash your hands after picking me up, especially if you eat just after holding me.

15

The Corn Snake

Snakes Alive!

If you think all snakes are dangerous creatures, get to know me, a corn snake, and I'll make you think again! Also known as a rat snake, I am a native of the southeastern United States. I am calm and tame and one of the most popular pet snakes in the world. Although I am often mistaken for the dangerous copperhead, I am not **venomous** and cannot hurt a human. I make an excellent pet for children, as long as there is an adult around to supervise cage cleaning and feeding.

In the snake world, I am the shrimp of the litter. As a **hatchling,** I might be between 9 and 14 inches (22 and 36 cm) in length; as an adult, I average between 2½ to 6 feet (1 to 2 m). I might live to be approximately 10 years old.

Open Wide!

Talk about big mouths! We snakes can stretch our jaws to ingest super-sized meals like a mouse or an egg.

Many people believe that reptiles will not outgrow their tanks. Not true! When I am a baby, I can live happily in a 10-gallon (38-liter) **aquarium.** I can even live in a plastic shoebox with holes punched on the sides, as long as the right light and heating is provided. However, when I reach the age of 3 or 4 and am fully grown, my housing needs will double. Then, nothing less than a 20-gallon (76-liter) aquarium will do.

Although I prefer to eat my food live, I am not a picky eater. It is safer for me to eat mice that have been frozen and then thawed to room temperature. An active, frightened mouse could really hurt me. How do *you* feel about a little mouse for dinner? I love it!

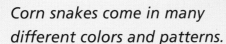

Corn snakes come in many different colors and patterns.

The Red-Eared Slider

Wet and Wonderful

Turtles make great house pets. A red-eared slider like me, an aquatic reptile from the southeastern United States, is particularly easy to care for. However, if you are looking for a pet you can play with, count me out. I am a solitary creature by nature. In the wild, I seek companionship only when it is time to breed. In captivity, I am wary of human touch and do not like to be held or cuddled. If I get spooked, I will slide deep into the water where you cannot reach me. That's why I am called a slider!

Unlike other reptiles, I rarely leave the water, except to bask in the sun on a nice warm rock for a few hours every day. The best home for me is a large aquarium, with plenty of water for swimming. A 10-gallon (38-liter) tank is sufficient for me when I am a baby.

As an adult, though, I will need a tank roughly 10 times that size. It's a good thing I grow slowly!

When I am fully grown, I can be as large as 10 inches (25 cm) long, and I can live to be between 30 and 40 years old. In other words, by the time you are an adult—perhaps with kids of your own—I might still be around. That's a long time to be responsible for a pet!

Mealtime

I will quickly learn to associate humans with food and will swim to the top of my tank if I expect a tasty snack. I like lettuce, sliced apples, berries, turnip greens, prepared turtle food, and even a little puppy chow! Be careful about letting unknown hands into my tank, though. I might bite the hand that feeds me if I don't know it.

The Right One for You

Reptiles are not great companions like dogs or a cats, and we're not bred for working, racing, or riding like horses. So what makes reptiles like me so fascinating? Some kids get hooked on reptiles the first time they see a snake crawl through the grass. Others choose us because they think we will not require as much time and attention as a furry, four-legged friend. They are wrong. Pets like me have many special needs.

Keep each animal's needs in mind when choosing which pet is right for you. For example, most turtles do not enjoy being handled.

Choosing the right reptile involves some investigation. You will need to find out how big I might get, what my temperament is like, and how much attention I require. Looks can be deceiving! A large snake may only need to be fed once a month, while a tiny lizard may need several daily feedings. I might like to be handled gently or might prefer not to be touched at all.

You will need to think about when I am active. If I am diurnal, you will notice that I am far more active when my cage is lit than when it is dark. If I am nocturnal, I like to sleep all day and come out only at night.

My eating habits vary by species, so think about what I eat before you bring me home. Some reptiles eat only vegetables and plants, but some of us eat meat. If you do not like handling live bugs or little white mice, then I may not be the right pet for you!

Reptiles make good pets because:
▶ We do well in apartments or small spaces.
▶ We are very clean.
▶ Our care is relatively inexpensive.
▶ We are beautiful and fascinating to watch.

My Favorite Things

Once you have chosen me as your pet, you should start assembling the things I need. You will need to think about where I will live. Would I prefer a simple shoebox, a wire mesh cage, a **terrarium,** or an aquarium?

Choose the home that will provide the best environment, lighting, humidity, and temperature for me. Wire cages fitted with wire mesh cloth make good homes for larger lizards, chameleons, and snakes. Terrariums and aquariums are a good choice for most geckos and turtles. Reproducing my natural environment will make me feel right at home in my new surroundings.

An aquarium makes a good home for a turtle. Decorate with rocks, plants, and other items found in a turtle's natural environment.

Do not forget to decorate. Depending on my species, I might like to climb, hide, or even swim!

I like a special place for eating, and another for resting. To keep my home clean, cover the bottom of the cage with bedding such as shredded newspaper, cypress mulch, sand, moss, wood shavings, feed pellets, or grasses and bark, depending on my species. Check my bedding regularly, and replace it when it gets soiled.

Leave Me Alone!

Reptiles like me prefer to live alone, which is why we do not get lonely the way humans sometimes can. Some of us can live together, but never keep two adult male lizards in the same cage. Adult male lizards are so aggressive that they will fight each other—sometimes to the death—when they come into contact.

Reptile Speak

Tails and Tongues

Unlike dogs that bark, cats that meow, and birds that chirp, most of us cannot speak at all. So how do you know what I am thinking? Watch carefully! Each of us has different ways of showing you what's on our minds.

Bobbing Beardies

Beardies like me love interacting with people and each other, and we use body language to communicate. When I bob my head up and down, I am asking, "Who is the boss here?" Waving my arms and bowing is a sign of **submission.** If I raise my tail, I am especially alert or something has caught my eye.

Say What?

Geckos like me are the only reptiles that can "speak." I will chirp or make a clicking sound when I am distressed. Although I cannot hear my own voice, the sounds I make can be heard by humans as well as other animals.

Don't worry if I seem to sleep a lot. Sleeping is normal behavior for me. In cooler weather, I may sleep a little more and eat a little less, just as I would do in the wild. However, if I am sleeping much more than usual, refusing to eat, and am not responding to you the way I usually do, I may be letting you know that I don't feel well. Visit a veterinarian and report any changes you observe in my behavior.

Tongue Talk

When something such as food, another snake, your hand, or even a new addition to my habitat attracts my attention, I will flick my powerful tongue in and out of my mouth. This expresses my curiosity.

Gearing Up

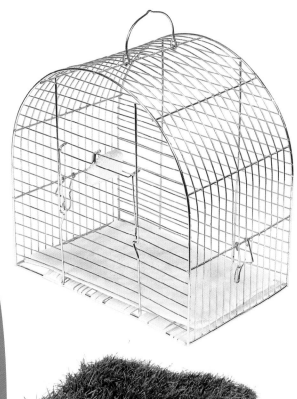

Your local pet store will be able to help you find everything you need to keep me happy and healthy. These are some of the most important items.

Caging: Choose a home for me that allows me plenty of room to move around—and don't forget to plan for all the growing I'll be doing! You might choose a wire mesh cage, a terrarium, or an aquarium, depending on my species.

Bedding: Cover the bottom of my cage with bedding such as shredded newspaper, cypress mulch, sand, moss wood shavings, feed pellets, or grasses and bark, depending on my species.

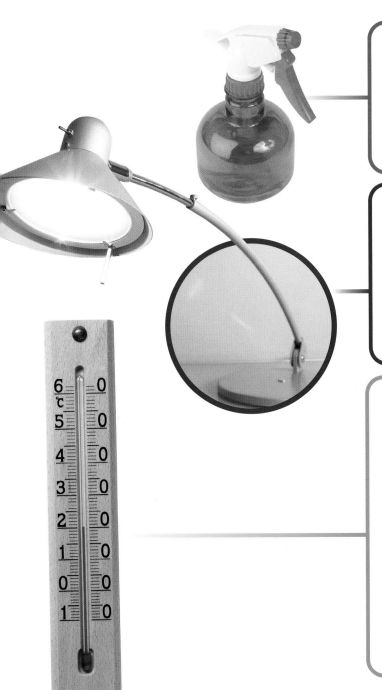

Water: My water supply should always be fresh and presented in a form that is closest to how I would get it in my natural environment. For some of us, this may mean spraying leaves in a cage; for others it may mean a water dish.

Light: I generally need 10 to 12 hours of daylight and prefer natural sunlight, if possible. Those of us who do not eat meat generally require a source of **ultraviolet light,** and those of us who are nocturnal need a good place to hide during the day.

Heat: You will need a thermometer to check and maintain the heat in my cage. Different reptiles have different heat requirements, and heat sources can also vary. A standard lightbulb may provide enough heat for some reptiles, but I may also need a heating pad, a heating rock, or a ceramic lightbulb to maintain my correct body temperature. Always place my heat source at one end of the cage so I can choose to be near it or away from it.

Fun Facts Scales and Tails

Double Threat

Some snakes are born with two heads. They can live happily together for a while—until one head eats the other!

Dinner, Anyone?

Hungry for a bite? When the alligator snapping turtle wants a snack, it attracts fish by opening its jaws and wiggling a special **appendage** in its mouth that looks like a worm.

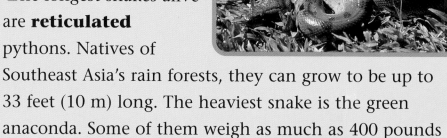

All-Purpose Alligator

Chinese medicine recommends using powdered alligator tail to cure anything from warts to lovesickness.

Super-Sized Snakes

The longest snakes alive are **reticulated** pythons. Natives of Southeast Asia's rain forests, they can grow to be up to 33 feet (10 m) long. The heaviest snake is the green anaconda. Some of them weigh as much as 400 pounds (180 kg)—the weight of two average-sized men!

Leaping Lizards!

A Komodo dragon that measured 10 feet (3 m) from head to tail holds the official record for world's largest lizard. A single Komodo dragon can weigh as much as 365 pounds (165 kilograms)!

Senior Citizens

Did you know that turtles can outlive humans? Galapagos tortoises can live to be 150 years old, making them the longest-lived reptiles. The North American box turtle can live up to 120 years, and the spur-thighed tortoises in Europe also survive over 100 years.

Important Dates Timeline

340M B.C. — **250M B.C.** — **5TH CENTURY A.D.** — **1519** — **1825** — **1871** — **1926** — **1992** — **1998** — **2002**

340 million B.C.
The first reptiles appear on Earth during the Carboniferous period. The earliest known reptile is called Westlothiana and looks a lot like a modern day lizard.

250 million B.C.
Turtles, tortoises, and terrapins make their debut, making them the oldest living group in the reptile family.

5th century A.D.
The legend is first told that St. Patrick drove all the snakes from Ireland.

1519 The Aztecs mistake the Spanish treasure seeker Cortes for "Quetzalcoatl," the plumed serpent, known as the "Divine King of the City of Gods."

1825 The dinosaur Iguanodon receives its name because its teeth, found in 1822, resemble those of a modern iguana. The dinosaur teeth were much bigger, of course.

1871 The first sighting of Nessie, the Loch Ness Monster, is recorded in Northern Scotland. Nessie is said to be 25 to 30 feet (8 to 9 meters) long and is called the "grandmother of all reptiles."

1926 An expedition to the Indonesian island of Komodo yields the first specimens of the world's largest and fiercest reptile — the Komodo dragon.

1992 "The Crocodile Hunter," starring Steve Irwin, debuts as a documentary in Australia. It is so popular that it leads to the creation of the hit TV shows "Crocodile Hunter" and "Croc Files."

1998 Franklin the Turtle steps off the printed page and onto Saturday morning TV in cartoons based on the popular picture books by Paulette Bourgeois and Brenda Clark.

2002 Thirty river terrapin hatchlings are released into the wild in Cambodia. These hatchlings, harvested from endangered adults first discovered in 2001, are designated "royal turtle guards" and have their own guards to protect their nesting sites.

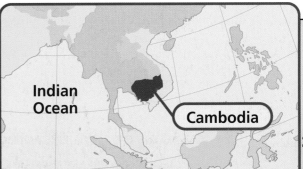

Indian Ocean

Cambodia

Words to Know

amphibians: a group of cold-blooded animals with backbones and moist, scaleless skin who usually live in or near water

appendage: an external body part, such as an arm or leg

aquarium: a tank or bowl filled with water for keeping underwater animals

captivity: kept without freedom

cone: a receptor cell in the eye that functions in color vision

diurnal: active mainly in the daytime

gharials: large, long-snouted reptiles from India related to crocodiles

hatchling: a baby animal that emerges from an egg

Jacobson's organ: a sense organ in a reptile's mouth used for smelling and tasting

keratin: a protein found in human nails and reptile scales

nocturnal: active mainly at night

orders: animal groups that contain one or more families

receptors: cells or groups of cells that receive sensory information

reptiles: cold-blooded, air-breathing animals that include alligators, crocodiles, lizards, snakes, and turtles

reticulated: marked in a way that forms a pattern

savannas: tropical or subtropical grasslands that contain scattered trees

submission: the act of surrendering power

terrapins: web-footed turtles that live in water

terrarium: a habitat with plants and some water for keeping semi-aquatic animals

tuataras: large, spiny, lizardlike reptiles

ultraviolet light: a powerful kind of light that cannot be seen by the human eye

venomous: poisonous

Where to Learn More

AT THE LIBRARY

Bartlett, Patricia. *Reptiles & Amphibians for Dummies*. New York: Wiley Publishing, Inc., 2003.

Holland, Simon. *Reptiles*. New York: Dorling Kindersley, 2002.

Ling, Mary, and Mary Atkinson. *The Snake Book*. New York: Dorling Kindersley, 2000.

St. Remy Media, Inc. *Reptiles & Amphibians*. New York: Discovery Communications, Inc., 2000.

Wilke, Harmut. *My Turtle and Me*. Hauppauge, N.Y.: Barron's Educational Series, 2002.

ON THE WEB

For more information on reptiles, use FactHound to track down Web sites related to this book.

1. Go to *www.facthound.com*

2. Type in a search word related to this book or this book ID: 0756506999.

3. Click on the *Fetch It* button.

Your trusty FactHound will fetch the best Web sites for you!

ON THE ROAD

American Museum of Natural History
Hall of Reptiles and Amphibians
Central Park West at 79th St.
New York, NY 10024
212/769-5100

Everglades National Park
40001 State Road 9336
Homestead, FL 33034
305/242-7700

Lincoln Park Zoo
Regenstein Reptile House
2001 N. Clark St.
Chicago, IL 60614
312/742-2000

Long Island Reptile Museum
70 Broadway
Hicksville, NY 11801
516/931-1500

Woodland Park Zoo
5500 Phinney Ave. N.
Seattle, WA 98103
206/684-4800

INDEX

ABOUT THE AUTHOR

Beth Gruber has worked in children's publishing for almost 20 years as an author, editor, and reviewer of many books for young readers. She also interviews other authors and TV show creators who write for children. Beth is a graduate of the NYU School of Journalism. Her passions are writing and reading. She lives in New York City with her 15-year-old Yorkshire terrier named Kozo.